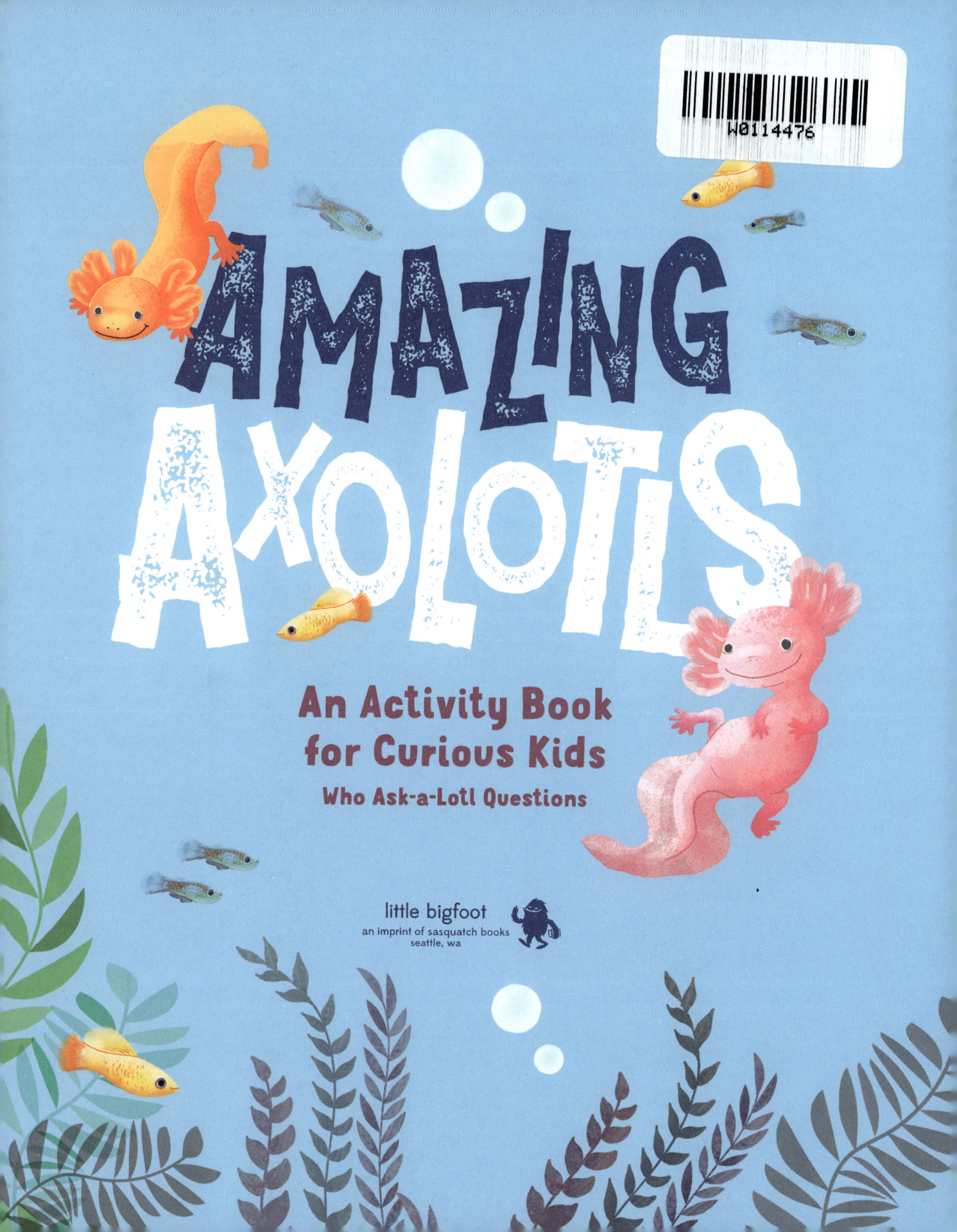

AMAZING AXOLOTLS

An Activity Book for Curious Kids

Who Ask-a-Lotl Questions

little bigfoot
an imprint of sasquatch books
seattle, wa

Printed in Colombia

LITTLE BIGFOOT with colophon is a registered trademark of Blue Star Press, LLC

Design and illustration by Moxey Creative Ltd.

9 8 7 6 5 4 3 2 1

The authorized representative in the EU for product safety and compliance is
Authorised Rep Compliance Ltd., Ground Floor, 71 Lower Baggot Street,
Dublin D02 P593, Ireland. www.arccompliance.com

A catalog record for this book is available from
the Library of Congress upon request.

ISBN: 978-1-63217-630-1

Sasquatch Books
1325 Fourth Avenue, Suite 1025
Seattle, WA 98101

SasquatchBooks.com

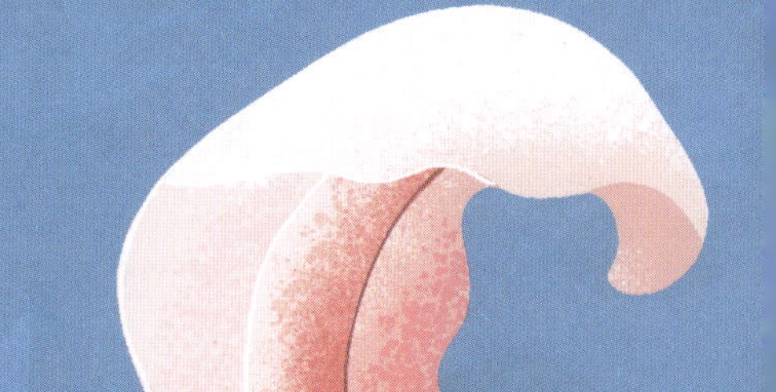

CONTENTS

ALL ABOUT AXOLOTLS

Axolotls are awesome animals. They have a cool name with an "x" in the middle of it. You say it like this: ack-suh-LAH-tuhl. They have adorable smiles on their faces all the time (unless, of course, they happen to be upside down).

Even though they have gills, axolotls still develop lungs.

Axolotls have teeny tiny teeth, but they don't use them to chew.

These fascinating creatures also have the rare ability to regrow their own body parts, from their toes to their brain!

Axolotls are nocturnal like bats and frogs. They sleep during the day and play and hunt at night.

HOW TO DRAW AN AXOLOTL

Step 1

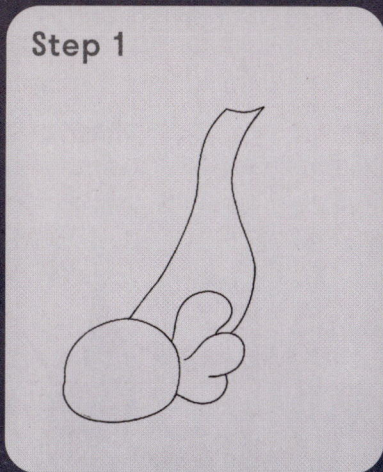

Step 2

Step 3

Step 4

DRAW YOUR OWN!

THE HISTORY OF AXOLOTLS

Did you know that axolotls have a name that comes from an ancient language? The Aztec people who lived in Mexico long ago had a god named Xolotl (say: SHOW-lotl). Xolotl was the god of fire, lightning, and dogs. The word "axolotl" comes from the Aztec words meaning "water dog."

Scientists believe axolotls have been around for a super long time—10,000 years! But their ancestors are even older, going back millions of years. Axolotls originally come from Mexico, where they lived in special lakes called Xochimilco (say: so-chee-MILL-ko) and Chalco.

For a long time, axolotls only lived in these lakes. But about 150 years ago, a person from Europe took an axolotl to a city called Paris. People in Europe thought axolotls were really cool and started keeping them as pets. Now, people all over the world love having pet axolotls!

LAKE TEXCOCO

LAKE XOCHIMILCO

LAKE CHALCO

VALLEY OF MEXICO, CIRCA 1855

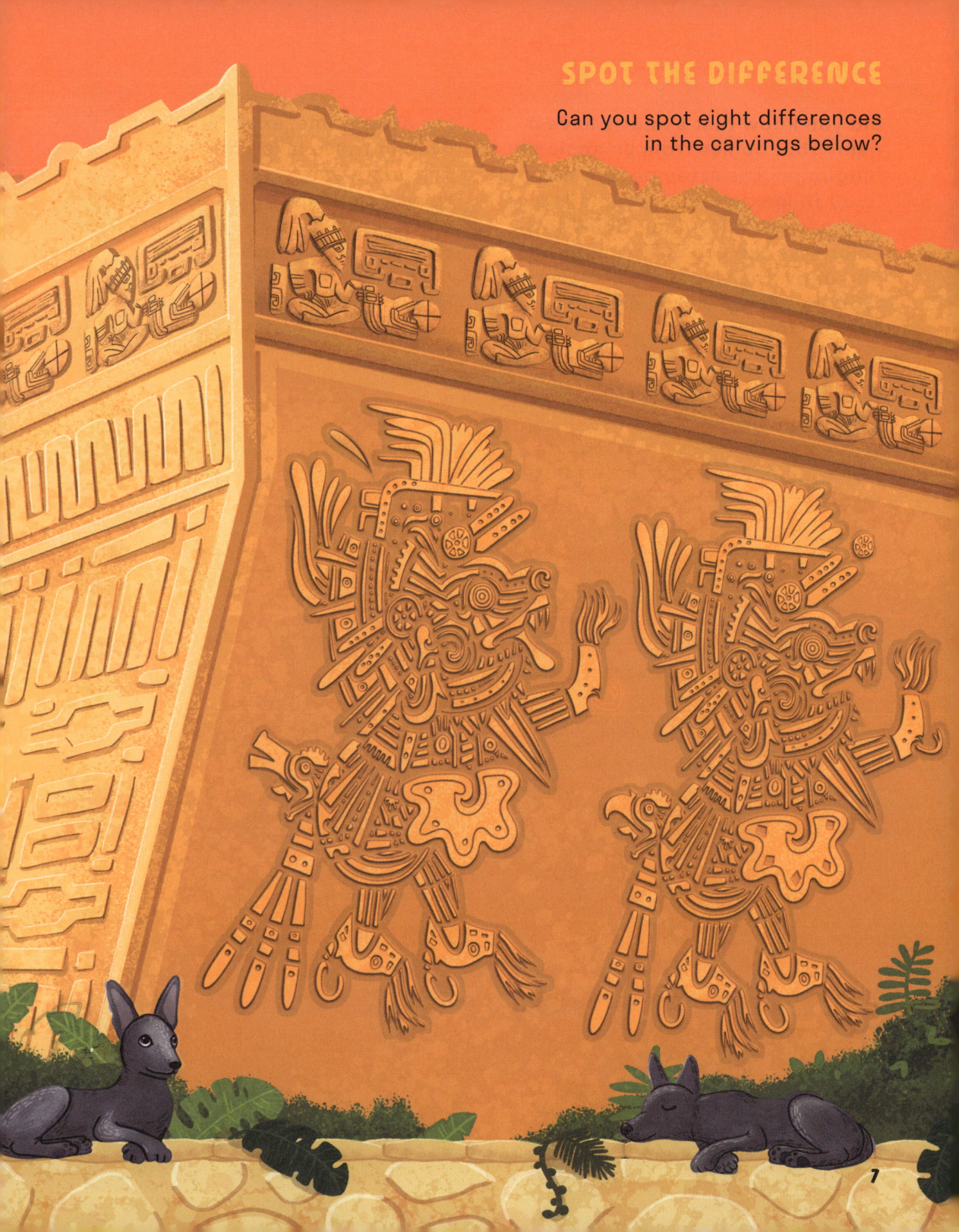

LOST AXOLOTL

This little axolotl is lost and needs to find its home fast! Can you figure out how to get it home safely?

START

END

```
E N W A T E R D O G
N N O N T S A N T N
W E D C R Z M Q F O
E Z O A T X Q I W T
B M Z T N U W G L E
B N W A O G R D O E
E L L H Y N E N T T
D U Z Y V G I R A H
J A H G O C M C E L
C A R N I V O R E D
```

FACT-FINDING MISSION

How well do you know the axolotl? It's time to find out. Find all seven facts about axolotls in the word search below. Answers can be found down, across, or diagonally.

SMILE

WATER DOG

WEBBED

NEOTONIC

NOCTURNAL

ENDANGERED

CARNIVORE

CLOSE RELATIVES

WHAT IS AN AMPHIBIAN?

Did you know that axolotls have some pretty cool cousins? They belong to a group of animals called amphibians. Amphibians are awesome because they can live both in water and on land!

Most amphibians start their lives in water and then grow up to live on land. It's like they have a secret superpower—they can completely change their bodies as they grow up! Baby frogs, called tadpoles, even breathe underwater using gills. But when they turn into adult frogs, they lose their gills and breathe with lungs instead. Scientists call this amazing change "metamorphosis."

But axolotls are a special kind of amphibian. They never fully change into land dwellers. Even as adults, they keep some of their baby features, like gills, and spend their whole lives underwater. It's like they're forever young!

Amphibians come in all shapes and sizes—some have smooth, slimy skin, while others have hairy or scaly skin. And they come in so many different colors! From tiny golden frogs to giant brown salamanders, the world of amphibians is full of surprises.

EGG   **LARVAL STAGE**   **ADULT**

Direct Developers Single habitat: Land

Viviparous Single habitat: Land

Paedomorphic Single habitat: Water

Biphasic Two habitats: Water and land

Flying Frog
Title: Coolest amphibian
Skill: Can achieve gliding flight

Golden Poison Dart Frog
Title: Most poisonous amphibian
Capability: Could kill 10-20 adult humans

Natterjack Toad
Title: Loudest in Europe
Distance heard: A mile

Nauta Salamander
Title: Fastest amphibian
Speeds reached: 15 mph

Coqui Frog
Title: Loudest worldwide
Decibels: 100

The Olm
Title: Longest-living amphibian
Predicted max lifespan: More than 100 years

Brazilian Flea Toad
Title: Smallest amphibian
Size: 7mm

Chinese Giant Salamander
Title: Largest amphibian
Size: 6ft

AMPHIBIAN FACTS & STATS

- Scientific name: *Amphibia*

- More than 8,000 known species

- Live almost everywhere except Antarctica

- Most go through metamorphosis as they grow

- All live near water

- Some can secrete toxins through their skin

THE CLASSES

There are three main types of amphibians: frogs and toads, salamanders and newts, and caecilians (say: see-SILL-ee-ens). Axolotls are part of the salamander group.

Frogs and toads are the bouncy acrobats of the amphibian world! They have powerful back legs for leaping and smooth, slimy skin. Some toads have skin that's bumpy and drier. But be careful—all toads have poisonous skin. Talk about a wild defense!

Caecilians are the oddballs of the amphibian family. They look like a mix between worms and snakes, with long, skinny bodies that are covered in tiny scales. They can dig tunnels underground like mini excavators.

Salamanders and newts are like the masters of disguise among amphibians—hard to spot because they look so much like lizards. There are around 800 kinds of salamanders in all sorts of colors, shapes, and sizes. Some are super small, and others are massive. A few can even create their own night lights!

PLAYING DEFENSE

Amphibians have some mind-blowing ways to keep themselves safe from danger. You can think of them as animal magicians! The poison dart frog's bright colors are like a big "Stay Away!" sign for predators. Fire salamanders ooze sticky goo that can make other animals really sick. And the mimic poison frog is a sneaky copycat, looking just like other poisonous frogs to trick hungry predators.

MATCH IT UP!

Now that you know a ton of facts about amphibians, it's time for you to show off. Read the clues below and match them with the correct amphibian pictured below. For an extra challenge, try timing yourself!

1. After metamorphosis, this animal will become a frog.

2. This amphibian has bumpy skin.

3. This amphibian is NOT a lizard.

4. This amphibian is poisonous.

5. This amphibian is round and venomous.

CRACKING UP

No one loves a good joke more than the axolotl, right? You can tell because it's always smiling—ha!

Here's a joke for you to crack: Use the secret cipher below to fill in the blanks with the correct letters and find the answer!

Why is the axolotl the most curious amphibian?

SECRET CODE

A 1 B 2 C 3 D 4 E 5 F 6 G 7 H 8
I 9 J 10 K 11 L 12 M 13 N 14 O 15 P 16
Q 17 R 18 S 19 T 20 U 21 V 22 W 23 X 24 Y 25 Z 26

$\overline{20}$ $\overline{8}$ $\overline{5}$ $\overline{25}$

$\overline{1}$ $\overline{24}$ $\overline{15}$ $\overline{12}$ $\overline{15}$ $\overline{20}$ $\overline{12}$

$\overline{17}$ $\overline{21}$ $\overline{5}$ $\overline{19}$ $\overline{20}$ $\overline{9}$ $\overline{15}$ $\overline{14}$ $\overline{19}$

SEEK & FIND

Can you find the 10 axolotls in this freshwater lake? Level up by trying to find the amphibians to the right, too.

Salamander **Frog** **Caecilian** **Toad** **Carp** **Tadpoles**

THE ANATOMY OF THE AXOLOTL

AXOLOTLS INSIDE AND OUT

Axolotls are famous for their cute, smiling faces. But there's more to these adorable amphibians than meets the eye!

Axolotls are neotenic, which means they keep their young features like gills and fins even as adults. This is why they can spend their whole lives underwater.

INSIDE

Axolotls have:

- Three pairs of feathery gills to breathe
- A long dorsal fin to swim up to 10 miles per hour
- Four legs with webbed feet to walk on land
- A three-chambered heart, like other amphibians

Heart

Gills

Dorsal Fin

Heart

BREATHING

Axolotls breathe through three organs: gills, skin, and lungs. Their outside gills have special fibers that also help catch food. Along the sides of their body are costal grooves with nerves and blood vessels to help oxygen flow.

LEGS

Axolotls have four legs—two in front, two in back. Their front feet have four toes, and their back feet have five. These help them move around in water and on land.

AXOLOTL SENSES

Like their eyesight, an axolotl's hearing isn't great. Loud noises can even make them temporarily deaf! But they make up for it with an amazing sense of smell, which helps them find food. They can also detect changes in water movement and vibrations.

EARS

An axolotl's hearing is pretty sensitive, but no records are being broken. Loud sounds can stress them out or make them lose hearing for a bit.

NEUROMASTS

Axolotls have a special sense that detects changes in water movement and vibrations—kind of like a superpower! It's called the lateral line and runs along the sides of their head and body.

EYES & NOSE

Similar to dogs, axolotls have an incredible sense of smell in order to locate food. But their eyesight? Not so great. Their lidless eyes don't work well and are very sensitive to bright light.

THE POWER OF REGENERATION

One of the coolest things about axolotls is their ability to regrow body parts! They can regrow tails, legs, gills, eyes, and even parts of their brain, heart, and lungs. Some regrowth happens super fast, in just weeks, while other parts can take a few months.

When an axolotl gets hurt, its body makes special cells called blastema. These cells work together like a super-hero team to regrow the missing parts. They turn into all the different cells needed, like skin, bone, and more. Axolotls make it look so easy!

Scientists are amazed by axolotls' regenerative powers. They hope that studying these awesome creatures might lead to new ways to help humans heal faster and better in the future. Wouldn't that be incredible?

Regeneration: Step 1

Step 2

Step 3

Step 4

Step 5

CROSSWORD PUZZLE

Read the clues below and write the answers in the correct spots—down or across!

CLUES ACROSS

2. These indents line the axolotl's ribs on both sides of its body

5. These webs are for swimming and walking

6. Axolotls spend their entire lives here

7. These whites don't work the way they should

8. Axolotls use these to breathe underwater

CLUES DOWN

1. This land animal's sense of smell is strong, just like the axolotl's

3. This helps axolotls sense when water is moving

4. This axolotl organ has three chambers

THE NOSE KNOWS

Navigate the dark lake bottom and help this hungry axolotl find food! Use your nose to follow the scent trail through the maze to the tasty treat. Hurry, your tummy's rumbling!

START

END

THE AXOLOTL SCRAMBLE

Can you unscramble all the scrambled axolotl words below? Write the correct words in the blank spaces below.

WORD BANK

REGENERATION   ALBINO

INACTIVE   ELECTRIC

SENSES   FIN

LIDLESS   PREDATOR

1. R E A R P O T
2. L I B A O N
3. D L S I L E S
4. C I V E A T I N
5. R E G E N R A T I O N
6. N E S S E S
7. N I F
8. L E E R T I C

1. _ _ _ _ _ _ _ _

2. _ _ _ _ _ _

3. _ _ _ _ _ _ _

4. _ _ _ _ _ _ _ _

5. _ _ _ _ _ _ _ _ _ _ _ _

6. _ _ _ _ _ _

7. _ _ _

8. _ _ _ _ _ _ _ _

21

LIFE FOR AN AXOLOTL

It may not look like it, but an axolotl actually goes through five different stages of growth during its life. Their metamorphoses are subtle. Still, if you look closely, you'll start to see it clearly.

STAGE 1: EGG TO EMBRYO →

Axolotls begin as eggs, like most amphibians. The embryo, surrounded by a jelly-like substance, starts to grow and develop. Its body and tail form, and gills and costal grooves appear.

STAGE 2: HATCHLING →

The jelly-like substance releases the larva, called a hatchling. At first, the hatchling is transparent, but as it grows, its skin thickens and it develops a longer body and flatter tail.

← STAGE 5: MATURE

Around one year of age, axolotls reach maturity and can reproduce. They continue to grow to full size over about two years but retain a youthful appearance.

STAGE 3: YOUNG JUVENILE

During this short stage, juvenile axolotls continue to grow. The rate of growth depends on food consumption. A key milestone: front legs!

STAGE 4: LATE JUVENILE

While most amphibians lose larval features at this stage, axolotls retain them due to neoteny. Key development in this five-month stage: hind legs.

Axolotls have incredibly sensitive skin. Even the gentlest human touch can irritate them.

Axolotl eggs aren't guarded by parents.

Axolotl hatchlings are so transparent, you can see their organs!

Axolotls lay 200 to 300 eggs at a time, but can lay up to 1,000! This helps them survive in the wild.

Some rare axolotls, like the Gollum axolotl, go through metamorphosis and become land dwellers as adults.

THE CUTEST LONER

Axolotls are intelligent and curious creatures who love exploring their environment. They seek out food and sneaky hiding spots for hunting or protection.

Despite their smiles, axolotls prefer solitude over company. They don't really engage with each other since they lack developed communication methods. In fact, axolotls don't even have vocal cords—the only sounds they make are gulps of air and water.

Axolotls may be small, but they can be quite aggressive. They are territorial and will fight over space and food, even resorting to cannibalism if resources are scarce. While axolotls aren't their preferred prey, they will eat each other in a pinch!

FACT-FINDING MISSION

Can you find all eight facts about axolotl behaviors in the word search below? Answers can be found down, across, or diagonally.

D	N	R	C	P	V	I	E	Z	H	R	N	A	C	I
K	Z	W	O	U	U	U	P	C	Y	K	E	Z	L	H
S	K	I	V	Q	R	X	Q	E	X	N	P	P	J	C
M	A	L	O	N	E	I	V	L	N	A	B	F	D	T
A	R	T	H	C	Y	K	O	V	A	L	N	A	Y	Y
R	Z	C	D	X	J	O	A	U	X	R	N	L	K	U
T	M	C	T	M	I	P	K	B	S	T	V	F	H	R
M	P	A	J	A	G	V	B	K	I	S	Q	A	A	O
S	E	N	S	I	T	I	V	E	S	K	I	N	T	J
D	Z	N	F	Z	Q	D	R	R	K	F	S	H	C	U
Y	D	I	C	P	Y	N	O	J	M	K	O	X	H	C
O	Q	B	T	I	B	S	X	A	J	O	N	B	L	M
Q	C	A	G	G	R	E	S	S	I	V	E	J	I	K
C	N	L	S	B	F	R	P	P	F	V	X	H	N	P
F	P	R	Q	B	L	M	I	U	O	Z	Z	B	G	L

WORD BANK

- CANNIBAL
- LARVA
- CURIOUS
- AGGRESSIVE
- HATCHLING
- SENSITIVE SKIN
- ALONE
- SMART

MATCH IT UP!

You've learned so much about the axolotl's life cycle! Show off what you know by reading the clues below and matching them with the correct life cycle stages pictured on the right. For an extra challenge, try timing yourself!

1. This stage is when it all begins.

2. This stage is short but sweet, marked by the arrival of two new body parts.

3. This stage is about five months long.

4. In this stage, some organs are visible through the axolotl's see-through skin.

5. After about a year, axolotls look like this.

AXOLOTLS IN THEIR HABITAT

WHERE DO AXOLOTLS LIVE?

Axolotls are uniquely native to just two lakes in Mexico: Lake Xochimilco (so-chee-MEEL-koh) and Lake Chalco (CHAL-koh).

While these lakes used to be vast, spanning more than 77 square miles, they each have since shrunk to a series of smaller lakes and canals.

Despite their size, these freshwater habitats are perfect for cold-blooded axolotls, with clean, warm water around 60°F (15°C). However, any temperature changes can cause stress and sluggishness.

Being limited to only two lakes makes axolotls vulnerable, as they can't relocate like other amphibians. Sadly, their habitat faces many threats.

THREATS IN THE WILD

As Mexico City grew, pollution and draining of lakes harmed axolotls. Diseases, invasive species like carp, and overfishing for the food and pet trades also pose major risks.

Axolotls are now critically endangered, just two steps from extinction. Conservation efforts are crucial to protect these unique creatures and their fragile home.

- Axolotls are just two steps away from complete extinction on the endangered species scale.

- A scientific study revealed that axolotl populations dropped from around 6,000 per square kilometer in 1998 to an alarming 35 in recent years.

- When the Spanish invaded and conquered Mexico in the 1600s, they drained most of the lakes native to that area.

- Weather changes like flooding, heavy rain, and drought have also led to the drainage and drying up of the axolotl's natural habitat.

- Roasted axolotl is considered a delicacy in Mexico City.

LET'S CLEAN UP LAKE XOCHIMILCO!

Hey there, nature hero! Did you know that axolotls need our help to keep their home in Lake Xochimilco clean and healthy? Sadly, pollution from old bottles, tires, and trash makes it hard for these cute creatures to thrive.

But guess what? You have the power to make a difference! With a little creativity and care, we can transform this icky garbage into something beautiful. Are you ready to work some magic for the axolotls?

TRACE THE LINES TO TURN TRASH INTO TREASURE!

1. Grab your favorite pencil or marker and get ready to trace.

2. Look closely at each piece of trash. Can you spot the hidden creature waiting to come alive?

3. Carefully trace along the light gray lines to reveal the secret animal or plant.

4. Watch in wonder as empty bottles bloom into lovely lotuses, old tires spin into smiley turtles, and forgotten wrappers flutter into fantastic fish!

5. Color in your creations and see how you've transformed the lake from mucky to magnificent!

SEEK & FIND

Let's help clean up Lake Xochimilco for our little axolotl friends. Find all 10 items of garbage in the water. Challenge yourself by finding all 5 small fishing nets, too.

SPOT THE DIFFERENCE

There are lots of colourful boats floasting on lake Xochmilco.
Can you find eight differences between boat A and boat B above?

WHAT DO AXOLOTLS EAT

Now let's dive into the juicy stuff—FOOD! Axolotls are meat-eaters, chowing down on yummy critters like worms, slugs, and even small fish. They're not picky at all and will gobble up anything that fits in their mouth!

Live worms are an axolotl's favorite snack. They're packed with protein, which makes up 30 to 60% of an axolotl's diet. Young axolotls need to eat once a day, but adults can live off of a big meal every two to three days.

One of the coolest things about axolotls is how they hunt. They don't chase their prey—instead, they use their awesome sense of smell and ability to detect movements to ambush unsuspecting critters. When an axolotl smells some-thing tasty nearby, it pops out of its hiding spot for a surprise attack!

HOW DO AXOLOTLS EAT?

Axolotls have seriously wide mouths, but their tiny teeth aren't strong enough to chew. So how do they eat? By using suction power! They catch a prey with their teeth, then vacuum it up whole. Down the hatch it goes!

EAT OR BE EATEN!

In the wild, axolotls are both hunters and hunted. They used to be the top predators in their habitat, but now they have to watch out for bigger threats, like:

- Large birds (herons, egrets, storks) that can spot and scoop them up

- Fish (carp, tilapia) that compete with them for food and territory

- Aquatic insects that munch on axolotl eggs and babies

- Other axolotls that might eat them if food is scarce

Axolotls are smart hunters:

- They hide and ambush their prey, instead of chasing it

- They use their sense of smell and motion detection to hunt

- They open their mouths wide to suction food down whole

- Their stomachs are the size of their heads

- They burrow in mud for sneak attacks

SEEK & FIND

Can you find all ten axolotls hiding from their predators? Quick, before they get eaten! Level up your game by fnding the five animals shown at the top.

Egret

Water Beetle

Tilapia

Wood Stork

Bullfrog

CRACKING UP

It's time for another round of jokes and code-cracking. Use Morse code to find these punchlines.

1. What do you call a tiny axolotl?

_ _ _ _ _ _ _ _

2. What do you call an axolotl with lots of gills?

_ _ _ _ _ _ _ _ _ _ _ _ _ _

Fill in the blanks with the correct letters and find the answer!

SECRET CODE

AXOLOTLS AS PETS

DO AXOLOTLS MAKE GOOD PETS?

Are axolotls good pets? The answer is YES! These smiling salamanders are super cool and can make awesome friends.

Axolotls have become extremely popular as household pets. It is estimated that one million axolotls are kept as pets or in labs around the world, compared to fewer than one thousand in the wild. Axolotls that are bred outside their natural habitat do differ from their wild counterparts in some ways. For example, a pet axolotl released back into the wild could cause harm to the axolotls' ecosystem—or to other wild axolotls. If you follow these guidelines, you and your pet axolotl can have a very happy coexistence.

GETTING READY FOR AN AXOLOTL

Before bringing an axolotl home, you'll need follow these guidelines:

1. **Get a tank with a filter:** Fill it with clean water around 60 degrees (that's chilly!).

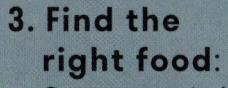

2. **Create a cozy home:** Add hiding spots like little caves or plants.

3. **Find the right food:** Get special food from a pet store that matches what they'd eat in the wild.

IMPORTANT AXOLOTL TIPS

- Keep your axolotl happy by tapping lightly on the glass to say hello.

- If you have more than one axolotl, give them separate tanks.

- Watch out! Axolotls can jump, so make sure your lid is tight.

HEADS UP!

It's not legal to have an axolotl as a pet everywhere. Check the rules in your area first. If you do get one for a pet, follow the guidelines, and take good care of them. You and your axolotl can be best buddies!

AXOLOTL HEALTH

Taking care of an axolotl is a big responsibility! These amazing underwater friends need a special home to stay healthy.

Axolotls love to be alone, which makes them perfect pets for people who want a calm, low-maintenance animal companion.

Keeping your axolotl happy means creating the perfect water home. They need clean, gentle water that isn't too strong—if the water flow is too powerful, your axolotl can get stressed and sick. Temperature matters too! A clean, carefully controlled tank keeps your little friend healthy and happy.

Here's the most incredible part: axolotls are like real-life superheroes! If they get a tiny injury, they can heal themselves in a magical way. In the right tank, they can even regrow parts of their body. Just remember, axolotls have super-sensitive skin, so look with your eyes, not your hands!

Melanoid

Leucistic

Wild Axolotls

Golden Albino

White Albino

AXOLOTL COLORING

Nature has painted axolotls in an amazing rainbow of colors! These underwater creatures come in three main color groups: blackish-brown, yellowish-orange, and shimmering gold or silver. But that's just the beginning of their colorful story!

MEET THE AXOLOTL COLOR CHAMPIONS:

White Albino: A see-through wonder with white eyes and a pink glow

Wild Axolotl: Grayish-green with speckles that tell a camouflage story

Golden Albino: Soft golden color that looks like sunshine underwater

Melanoid: Dark and mysterious, like a shadow moving through water

Leucistic: Pale with striking black eyes that seem to sparkle

Color the axolotls on the right however you want! Each axolotl is a one-of-a-kind masterpiece, with colors that make them special and amazing!

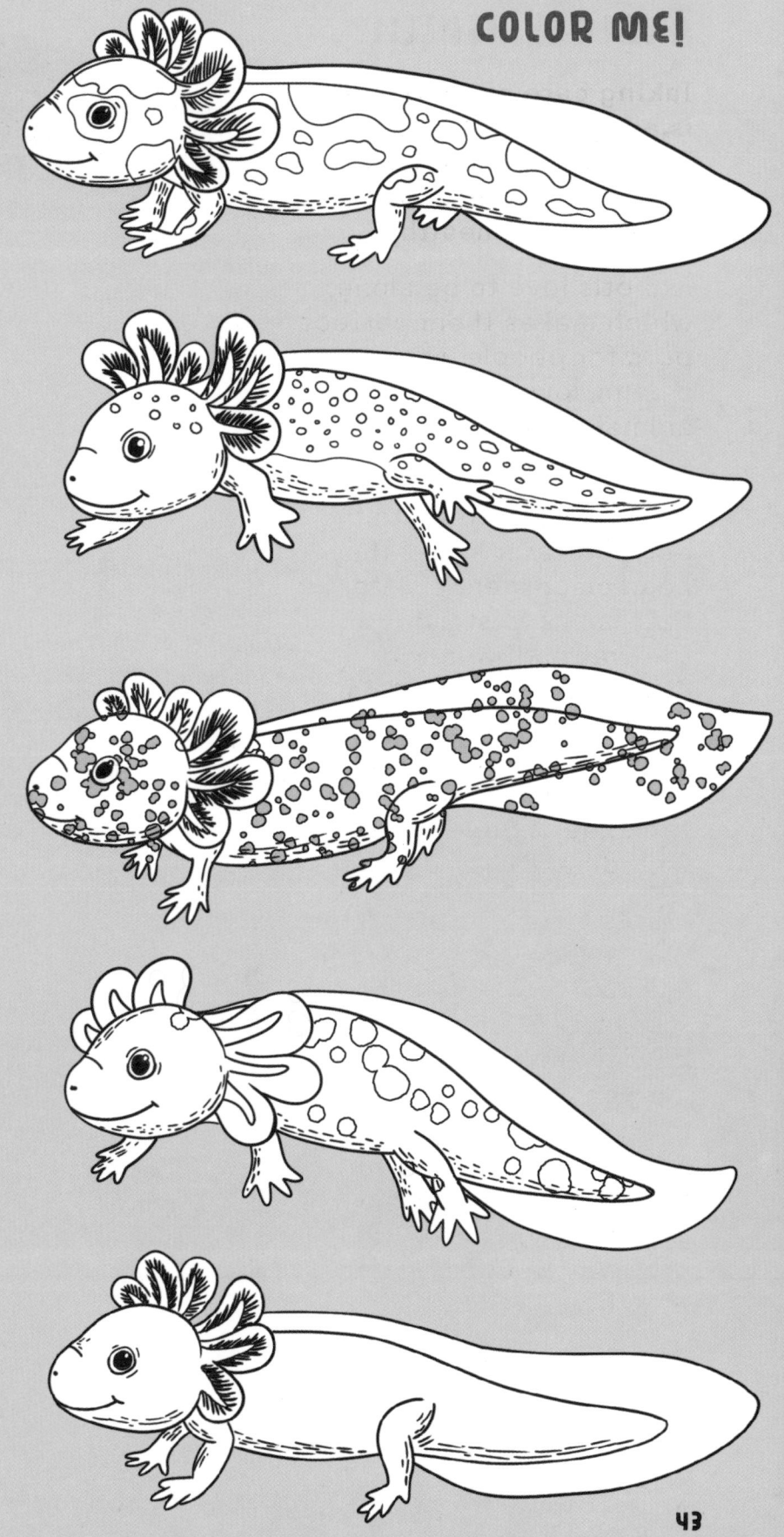

CROSSWORD PUZZLE

Are you ready to play again? Read the clues below and write the answers in the correct places on the puzzle. Answers go down and across.

ACROSS

1. Axolotl pets live inside one of these

3. This is the number of colors that are genetically natural in axolotls

4. Axolotls need a lot of this in their water

7. This is a major cause of health issues for axolotls

8. This unit measures the amount of acid in water

DOWN

2. It is illegal to have a pet axolotl in this Garden State

5. This color group is almost see-through

6. This kind of axolotl is mixed and isn't naturally occurring.

SPOT THE DIFFERENCE

Can you spot the eight differences between the two tanks below?

ANSWERS

PAGE 7

PAGE 8

PAGE 9

PAGE 13

PAGE 14

PAGE 15

PAGE 19

PAGE 20

1. PREDATOR
2. ALBINO
3. FINS
4. REGENERATION
5. SENSES
6. ACTIVE
7. LIDLESS
8. ELECTRIC

PAGE 21

PAGE 25

PAGE 26

PAGE 32

PAGE 33

PAGE 36-37

1. AN AXOLITL
2. A GILLIONAIRE

PAGES 38-39

PAGE 44

PAGE 45

GLOSSARY

Albino: An animal born without pigment in its skin, hair, or eyes. It typically looks pale and might have pink or red eyes.

Amphibian: A type of animal that can live both in water and on land.

Axolotl: A special kind of amphibian that stays in its baby form for life and lives underwater with fluffy-looking gills on its head.

Blastema: A group of special cells that helps animals grow back missing body parts, like a tail or a leg.

Cannibal: An animal that eats others of its own kind.

Embryo: An animal at a very early stage before it's born or hatched.

Endangered: A word used to describe animals that are in danger of disappearing forever.

Extinction: When a kind of animal or plant disappears and is gone forever.

Gill: A body part some animals use to breathe underwater, like fish and baby frogs.

Hatchling: A baby animal that recently came out of an egg.

Larva: An animal in its young form that looks very different from its adult form, like a caterpillar before it becomes a butterfly.

Metamorphosis: A big change in the way an animal looks as it grows, like when a tadpole turns into a frog.

Neotenic: A word used to describe an animal that keeps its baby features even after growing up, like axolotls keeping their gills.

Predator: An animal that hunts and eats other animals.

Regeneration: When an animal can grow back a lost body part, like a lizard growing a new tail.

Salamander: A small, slippery animal that looks like a mix between a lizard and a frog, and often lives in wet places.

Toxin: A poison made by animals, plants, or germs that can make others sick.